Did ~~You~~
LEIC~~ESTER~~

A MISCELLANY

Compiled by Julia Skinner
With particular reference to the work of Michael Kilburn

THE FRANCIS FRITH COLLECTION

www.francisfrith.com

Based on a book first published in the United Kingdom in 2006 by The Francis Frith Collection®

This edition published exclusively for Identity Books in 2010 ISBN 978-1-84589-408-5

British Library Cataloguing in Publication Data

Did You Know? Leicester - A Miscellany
Compiled by Julia Skinner
With particular reference to the work of Michael Kilburn

The Francis Frith Collection
Frith's Barn, Teffont,
Salisbury, Wiltshire SP3 5QP
Tel: +44 (0) 1722 716 376
Email: info@francisfrith.co.uk
www.francisfrith.com

Printed and bound in Malaysia

Front Cover: **LEICESTER, THE FOUNTAIN IN FRONT OF THE TOWN HALL c1955** L144074p

The colour-tinting is for illustrative purposes only, and is not intended to be historically accurate

CONTENTS

INTRODUCTION

The busy modern city of Leicester stands on historic foundations. It was the 'civitas', or capital, of a Celtic tribe, and was called Ratae Coritanorum by the Romans, who also had an important settlement here; the Jewry Wall is believed to date from AD130, and excavations have revealed a public bath and shops.

After the Norman Conquest a castle was built here, but it was destroyed in 1173, along with the rest of the town, during a rebellion against Henry II by two of his sons, Richard ('the Lionheart') and John. The Earl of Leicester joined the rebels, but the king won. The earl fled to France, and the king took a savage revenge against Leicester, leading to the deaths of many of the citizens. The earl was later allowed to return and rebuilt the castle, but all that survives is the motte and the Great Hall, which dates from the late 12th century. St Mary de Castro, the church of the castle, is basically Norman, and St Martin's Cathedral has its origins in a 13th-century church.

Even before the Industrial Revolution, Leicester had a thriving hosiery industry. When Daniel Defoe travelled around Britain in the 1720s he commented: 'Leicester is an ancient, large and populous town, containing about five parishes, and stands on the River Soar. They have considerable manufacture carried on here, and in several of the market towns round for weaving of stockings by frames, and one would scarce think it possible so small an article of trade could employ such multitudes of people as it does; for the whole county seems to be employed in it.' However, Leicester's development from a small county town into the sprawling industrial city of today was prompted by the construction of the Grand Union Canal in the 1790s, linking Leicester to London and Birmingham, and the coming of the railway in the 19th century. The census of 1801 showed Leicester's population to be around 17,000 people. The hosiery industry flourished, and Leicester continued to expand, aided by the successful boot and shoe and engineering industries. By 1901 the population had increased to around 212,000 people. Leicester

is renowned for its flamboyant Victorian architecture, some of the superb buildings of this period being the former Midland Bank (HSBC), the Turkey Cafe, and the Singer Building, and the richness of the city's history is reflected in its many museums.

In the 20th century Leicester suffered from war damage and industrial decline, but is now moving forward into the 21st century as a vibrant lively city with a large immigrant population, and an enviable reputation for intercultural harmony. Life in Leicester has been greatly enriched by the diversity of the festivals and cultures of its citizens, such as the Diwali Lights, the Caribbean Carnival and the fruit and vegetables from all over the world that can be found at Leicester Market, the largest covered market in Europe. One of the joys of visiting Leicester is the chance to eat in one of the city's famous Indian restaurants, many of which are to be found along Belgrave Road.

The story of Leicester is full of fascinating characters and events, of which this book can only provide a brief glimpse.

BELVOIR STREET c1949 L144017

LEICESTERSHIRE DIALECT
WORDS AND PHRASES

'Bungole' - cheese.

'Are kid' or 'mi chip' - my brother.

'Charlie's dead' - your petticoat is showing.

'Coddie' - foreman.

'Cotty' - tangled or untidy hair.

'The cut' - the canal.

'Duck's necks' - bottles of fizzy drinks.

'E's gorra chin on' - he's being sulky, or cross.

'Ginnel' - an alleyway or path.

'I ain't up Co'ville' - I can hear you, no need to shout.

'Jollop' - medicine.

'Mashin the tea' - brewing the tea.

'Necky Becky' - a nosey person.

'Puthering down with rain' - raining very heavily.

'Skants' - underwear.

'Snaps' - lunch, or a snack.

'Well, I'll go to the foot of our stairs' - that's really surprised me.

HAUNTED LEICESTER

The Abbey Pumping Station is said to be haunted by the ghost of an engineer who fell to his death from the top balcony into the engine room in the 19th century.

Staff at Newarke Houses Museum have reported feeling the presence of someone nearby, and visitors are told to look out for a glimpse of a mysterious cloaked figure.

In 1998 Belgrave Hall was the scene of a paranormal investigation after two figures in Victorian clothing were spotted on CCTV. They seemed to have come through a courtyard wall. After a number of tests, the investigators concluded that the images had been caused by falling leaves - but who knows…

The Black Dog Inn in Oadby is said to have its own ghost, possibly linked to an earlier use of the Long Skittle Alley as a morgue.

Leicester's most haunted building is the Guildhall, which boasts five ghosts. The most frequent visitor, though rarely seen, has been dubbed the White Lady, who moves heavy furniture around the library, and opens locked doors.

LEICESTER MISCELLANY

Leicester University is one of the city's modern landmarks. The School of Engineering was designed by James Stirling and James Gowan; it was completed in 1963 and won an architectural award for the use of aluminium in its construction.

Next time you are passing the HSBC Bank in the city centre, on the corner of Granby Street and Bishop Street, look out for the monsters which crawl over the walls of the building. These are the work of the stonemason Samuel Barfield, who often worked with the architect of the building, Joseph Goddard, who also designed the Clock Tower and the Thomas Cook Building. The building was originally the Leicestershire Bank, and was built in 1874 in Venetian-Gothic style with French pavilion roofs. It is one of the best examples of the superb Victorian architecture for which Leicester is famous.

Designed by Shirley Harrison in 1913, Leicester's De Montfort Hall is one of the Midlands' finest concert halls (see L144118 on page 50-51). The name of the building commemorates Simon de Montfort, the 1st Earl of Leicester, who led a successful revolt of the barons against Henry III. The parliament that de Montfort summoned in 1265 set a precedent for future relations between the English monarch and subjects.

The Abbey of St Mary de Pratis, which is laid out in the north-west angle of Abbey Park, was one of the largest in England of the Augustinian Order. It was founded in 1143 by Robert le Bossu, and was dissolved in 1538 after an unsuccessful attempt by the last abbot to withstand the suppression.

Did You Know?
LEICESTER
A MISCELLANY

THE CLOCK TOWER AND BELGRAVE GATE c1955 L144006

Tram wires and tracks are evident in photograph L144006 (above), of the Clock Tower and Belgrave Gate. With five important roads making this junction, it proved to be one of the most complicated tramway configurations in the world.

There are two war memorials in Victoria Park. Best known is the Memorial Arch, which commemorates the dead of the First World War and was designed by the great architect Sir Edwin Lutyens (L144028, page 15). The second memorial commemorates the American 82nd Airborne Division, who were based in Leicester prior to the D Day landings in 1944.

Thomas Cook started his successful travel business from a building overlooking Leicester's Clock Tower in 1841. A spectacular new front was added to the building in 1894, recording that from these offices Mr Thomas Cook arranged the world's first cheap day rail excursion (to Loughborough) in 1841, and went on to provide affordable travel for ordinary people, both at home and on the continent. Cook died in 1892, a stalwart of the Temperance Movement.

Closing the view south in photograph L144016 (below) is the former General Accident Building of 1932, which Nikolaus Pevsner rather unkindly summed up as 'a vile, impertinent lump'.

MARKET STREET 1949 L144016

THE RIVER SOAR BRIDGE c1955 L144063

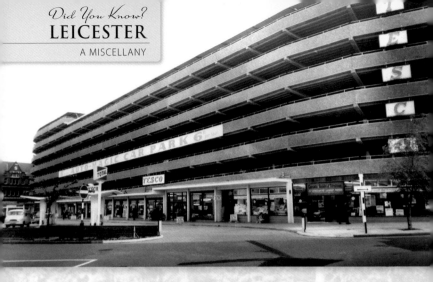

THE AUTO MAGIC CAR PARK, LEE CIRCLE c1965 L144087

Leicester's Auto Magic Car Park was one of the first multi-storey car parks of this size in the country, and was quite a talking point at the time. It was almost brand new at the time photograph L144087 (above) was taken, originally intended for use as a postcard of this exciting new development.

The name of Gallowtree Gate probably refers to the gallows which were sited at the top of London Road hill, close to its junction with Evington Lane. In the 15th century, Gallowtree Gate and Church Gate ran parallel with the east wall of the town and the town ditch.

In 1645, during the Civil War, Leicester was besieged and captured after a bitter struggle by Royalist forces, only to be retaken by Parliamentarians following the Royalist defeat at Naseby.

Gun-loops dating to the time of the Civil War in the 1640s can still be seen in the medieval wall in the garden of the Newarke Houses Museum.

Cavendish House in Abbey Park (L144088, below) was built c1600 by Henry Hastings, Earl of Huntingdon, using stone robbed from the remains of Leicester Abbey, but it was reduced to a skeletal ruin by fire 45 years later. The main front seen in the photograph is virtually all that remains; the house to the right is 19th-century.

CAVENDISH HOUSE, ABBEY PARK c1955 L144088

Early travellers to Leicester were not impressed. The diarist John Evelyne called it an 'old and ragged Citty…despicably built' in 1654, and a little later Daniel Defoe condemned it as 'an old stinking town'. The side-saddle traveller Celia Fiennes liked it better in 1698: 'Leicester town stands on the side of a little riseing ground tho' at a distance from the adjacent hills it looks low, but it's a good prospect; it has 4 gates, the streets are pretty large and well pitch'd, the Market place is a large space very handsome with a good Market Cross and Town Hall.'

A plaque on Bow Bridge records a supposed prophesy that was given to Richard III as he left Leicester on his way to his death at the battle of Bosworth in 1485. Richard's spur is said to have struck the parapet when crossing, causing a bystander to predict that his head would later do the same. This prophecy is supposed to have come true two days later, when the dead king's body was brought back to Leicester, dangling across a horse's back - as the horse crossed the bridge, the king's head did indeed hit the parapet. After public display in the Church of St Mary of the Annunciation in the Newarke, the king's body is believed to have been buried in the chapel of the Grey Friars. Legend says that Richard's bones were dug up at the Dissolution of the Monasteries in the 16th century and thrown over Bow Bridge, later to be buried on the banks of the Soar, and that a stone coffin, said to be Richard's, was used as a horse trough at the White Horse Inn, Gallowtree Gate.

THE WAR MEMORIAL, VICTORIA PARK
c1950 L144028

PRINCE RUPERT'S GATEWAY, CASTLE YARD c1955 L144071

During the 18th century turnpiking improved access by road, particularly to and from London, and in 1774 Leicester was opened up when its medieval gates were demolished.

The Church of St Mary de Castro (L144050, page 20), situated as its name implies within the medieval castle, was founded by Robert de Beaumont in 1107 as a secular college, but by c1143 it had been annexed to Leicester's large Augustinian abbey. Its spire was rebuilt in 1785 and the church was much restored in the 19th century. Inside the church are five very fine stone sedilia, or seats for the clergy, dating from the late 12th century.

Leicester is home to the Leicestershire Museum of Technology, which features a collection of 19th-century beam pumping engines; these can be seen working on 'steaming' days. There is also the largest collection of hosiery machinery in the world, reflecting the local importance of that industry.

The Church of St Nicholas is one of the oldest churches in England (L144054, below). It is Saxon in style and may have been built in the 7th century; some stone from the Roman town appears to have been used in its tower.

THE CHURCH OF ST NICHOLAS AND THE JEWRY WALL c1955 L144054

GRANBY STREET 1949 L144032

**PRINCE RUPERT'S GATEWAY AND
ST MARY DE CASTRO CHURCH c1955** L144050

St Martin's Church, with its fine broach spire of 1862, was raised to cathedral status in 1927. The 17th-century traveller Celia Fiennes was most impressed with the inside of the church: 'St Martin's Church which is one of the biggest (there is none very big and none fine) but here I saw Hyricks tomb who was Major of the town and was married to one wife 52 years, in all which time he buried neither man woman nor child tho' most tymes he had 20 in his family, his age was 79 and his widdow 97 at her death, she saw 142 of her posterity together'.

Leicester's Newarke Houses Museum is composed of two historic houses, Wygston's Chantry House and Skeffington House. Wygston's Chantry House was built c1511-12 by William Wygston, in his day Leicester's wealthiest citizen. It was the home of two chantry priests who sang masses for William's soul in the nearby (now demolished) church of St Mary of the Annunciation. The building originally had only two storeys but a third floor was added later in the 1500s. The house was restored in the 1950s, after war damage. It is the only Elizabethan urban gentry house that survives in Leicestershire.

One of the folktales associated with Leicester is the story of Black Annis, who lived in the Dane Hills area. Black Annis was a witch-like hag who would lie in wait in her cave for disobedient children who had strayed too far from home. Parents would use her to frighten their children into good behaviour, saying Black Annis would seize them, skin them alive and eat them up, scattering their bones around her cave and hanging their skins to dry on an old oak nearby.

Did You Know?
LEICESTER
A MISCELLANY

The magnificent East Window of St Martin's Cathedral is a monument to the dead of the First World War; its design makes much use of red, which sets the cathedral ablaze when the morning light streams through it. In the centre, Jesus is portrayed holding a starry heaven in his hand, whilst his foot rests on a bloody hell; around Him stand 8 angels, whose wings are depicted in red glass. The window also depicts St Martin, to whom the cathedral is dedicated, standing on the tail of a dragon, with St George standing on its head. A First World War soldier can also be found. The window is particularly significant in this cathedral, as the saint day of St Martin, the patron saint of the cathedral, is 11 November, Armistice Day.

New Walk, which runs from Welford Place in the city centre up to Granville Road opposite Victoria Park, is a tree-lined Georgian footway where all vehicles, including bicycles, have always been forbidden. The original purpose of New Walk was to allow pedestrians to walk from the town to the racecourse (in its earlier site at Victoria Park) away from the mess and mud on London Road. The footway has had several names: it was named Queen's Walk when it was first laid out in 1785, in honour of Queen Charlotte, wife of George III; later it became Ladies' Walk, and then the less romantic New Walk.

One of Leicester's most fascinating buildings is the Turkey Café, which can be found in Granby Street, between Halford Street and Rutland Street, and opposite Bishop Street. The architect was Arthur Wakerley, who later became Mayor of Leicester and also designed the Singer Building. The building boasts a number of portrayals of turkeys, on either side of the entrance and in a mosaic on the top floor.

ST MARTIN'S CATHEDRAL c1955 L144026

23

THE GREAT HALL, CASTLE YARD c1965 L144092

The Great Hall is all that remains of Leicester's castle, built by Robert, Earl of Leicester around 1150. It has been pared down from its original aisled form, and has been provided with what is basically a 17th-century range and brick front (L144092, above). It is now used as the Crown Court.

At the Peace of Wedmore in AD878 between the Danes and King Alfred, the two sides agreed to split the country into two areas of control. Leicester was absorbed into the Danelaw (the area under Danish control) as one of the Five Boroughs (the others were Stamford, Nottingham, Lincoln and nearby Derby).

As a means of preserving law and order in 16th-century Leicester, it was enacted that no person of whatever degree should be abroad in the streets after nine o'clock at night, except for the night watchmen and officers.

The Fielding Johnson Building (L144112, below) is somewhat incongruous among the more modern buildings of the University of Leicester. This brick faced symmetrical building with its linked pavilions was in its former life the Leicestershire Lunatic Asylum of 1837. This original use may be discernible in the closely-packed glazing bars to the ground storey windows of the pavilion.

THE FIELDING JOHNSON BUILDING, UNIVERSITY OF LEICESTER c1965 L144112

BELGRAVE GATE c1949 L144013

KIBWORTH HARCOURT, THE OLD MILL
c1955 K171033

Leicester was the venue in 1426 of the intriguingly named Parliament of Bats. The king at the time, Henry VI, was an infant, and there was great tension between the Duke of Gloucester, the king's uncle and regent, and Cardinal Beaufort, the Bishop of Winchester and off-and-on Lord Chancellor. The name comes from the fact that the members were forbidden by the Duke of Gloucester to carry swords into the parliament, but they were so concerned that violent disagreement might ensue that they armed themselves with clubs, or bats. This session of parliament also saw the infant king knighted in the church of St Mary de Castro.

Not far from Leicester, at Kibworth Harcourt, is the last post-mill in Leicestershire, dated 1711 (see opposite), which was last used in 1912. This type of mill predates tower and smock mills, utilising the simple principle of following the wind by revolving the body of the building round a fixed central post. These mills were weatherboarded for lightness. The mounds which often supported them can sometimes be clearly seen close to deserted or shrunken villages.

The line of New Walk actually follows the old Roman road, the Via Devana, which ran from Leicester to Colchester.

In 1612 a conduit was built to carry water from springs into the town, giving the name to Conduit Street.

In 1899 the line of the Great Central Railway opened; the line between Nottingham and London was formerly used for coal haulage. In the 20th century the line was unable to compete with the motorcar and by 1966 several sections were closed. Since 1969, however, enthusiasts have succeeded in reopening the section between Loughborough and Leicester, and several stations along the way have been restored.

The city's motto is 'Semper Eadem', which was the motto of Elizabeth I, who granted a royal charter to Leicester. It means 'always the same'.

Leicester is home to the National Space Centre, and the University of Leicester is one of the few universities in the UK to specialise in space science. The city had the first Space Shuttle Simulator outside the USA.

Did you know - that Leicester had the first roundabout in the UK?

THE TUDOR GATEHOUSE, CASTLE STREET
c1955 L144093

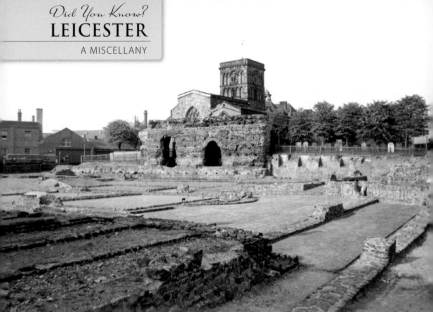

THE ROMAN REMAINS AND JEWRY WALL c1955   L144069

The remains of Ratae Coritanorum, a regional capital in Roman Britain, lie adjacent to the superb Saxon church of St Nicholas and are seen in the centre of photograph L144069 (above). The so-called Jewry Wall formed part of the exercise hall to the public bath. The forum and basilica were excavated by Kathleen Kenyon in the 1930s. The remains are situated at the top of the High Street.

Visitors can step back in time in the Guildhall museum, where they will find 'Crankie Gemmie' and 'Emma Smith', two of Leicester's notorious pick-pockets, lurking in the Victorian police cells.

Leicester grew rapidly in the 18th and 19th centuries, but it continued to be governed from its small medieval Guildhall until 1876. A visit to the Guildhall is worthwhile, to see the amazing 14th-century timbered Great Hall of the Corpus Christi Guild, a powerful guild of local businessmen and gentry. The Corporation bought the building in 1548 when the Guild was dissolved, for the sum of £25 15s 4d! Since then the Guildhall has had many uses, and survived calls for its demolition as an eyesore in the early 20th century, but is now in safe hands as a performance venue and museum. The Guildhall is also reputed to be Leicester's most haunted building, boasting a total of five different ghosts.

THE GUILDHALL, GUILDHALL LANE c1949 L144025

33

EASTGATES 1949 L144002

THE CLOCK TOWER AND GALLOWTREE GATE c1965 L144097

Leicester's Gothic Clock Tower was designed by local architect Joseph Goddard in 1868, and is decorated with pinnacles and canopies, along with representations of four Leicester worthies: Alderman Gabriel Newton, Simon de Montfort, William Wygston, and Sir Thomas White, one-time Mayor of Leicester and landlord of the nearby Horse and Trumpet.

Boot- and shoe-making boomed in Leicester in the 19th century. In 1831, 425 boot- and shoe-makers were recorded in the town; by 1861 there were 2,741. Several household names had factories in Leicester, among them Freeman, Hardy & Willis, and George Oliver.

The name 'Leicester' is believed to derive from the words 'castra (camp) of the Ligore', meaning 'dwellers on the River Legro' (which was an early name for the River Soar). In the early 10th century it was recorded as 'Ligeraceaste', or 'the town of the Ligor people'. By the time of the Domesday Book in the late 11th century the name of the settlement had become 'Ledecestre'.

Alfred Wakerley, who designed the Turkey Café in Granby Street, also designed the Singer Building in the High Street. He decorated this building with animals as well, representing various parts of the British Empire. These include a kangaroo (Australia), a bear (Canada), a tiger (India), an elephant (Burma), an ostrich (Africa) and a dromedary (Egypt).

GALLOWTREE GATE c1950 L144009

HUMBERSTONE GATE 1949 L144007

SPORTING LEICESTER

Belgrave-born Jenny Fletcher was a major star of women's swimming in the early 1900s. She was undefeated over four years from 1906-09, setting 11 new world records during this time. Her wins included 6 'Champion of England' medals, and an Olympic Gold Medal. She was inducted into the International Swimming Hall of Fame in 1971, with the inscription 'The World's First Great Woman Swimmer' above her picture. There is a plaque commemorating her achievements at Cossington Street pool.

Horse racing in the Leicester area is recorded as far back as 23 March 1603, the day before Elizabeth I died. Since then racing has taken place at various locations including Victoria Park, St Mary's Field, and the present course at Oadby. Highlights over the last 400 years include the first running of the Leicester Gold Cup in 1807, and Gordon Richards riding his first winner, Gay Lord, in 1921.

On 10 February 1923, England beat Ireland at rugby at Leicester's Welford Road ground. It was significant as being the last England home match played away from Twickenham until 1992, 69 years later. Another game played against Ireland, in 1984, saw seven Leicester players line up for their country, a club record.

Grace Road, Leicester, is the home of Leicestershire County Cricket Club. They have played there since 1877, and the ground is said to have the second largest playing area in the world.

FOOTBALL

During the 1974/75 season, seven Leicester City players played against Arsenal seven times. The teams played two League, 3 FA Cup and two League Cup matches. John Samuels, Steve Whitworth, Len Glover, Keith Weller, Steve Earl, Frank Worthington and Alan Birchenall all took part in all of the matches.

An ex-Leicester City player, Arthur Rowley, holds the record for the most goals scored by a player in League football. He scored 433 goals, 54 more than his nearest rival, Dixie Dean. 265 of those goals were scored for Leicester City, before Rowley left the club in 1958.

Another notable Leicester City record is that of goalkeeper Mark Wallington. He didn't miss a single match between 1975 and 1981.

One of Leicester's most famous sporting sons is Gary Lineker, born in the city in 1960. Gary had the honour of playing for Leicester City for seven years before joining Everton in the summer of 1985, and made his England debut in May 1984 against Scotland at Hampden Park. He became the first England international to win the World Cup Golden Boot in the 1986 World Cup tournament, and went on to captain England from 1990-92. He finished his career as England's second highest goal scorer, his final score of 48 being only one goal behind the record holder, Bobby Charlton. He is famous for never having been booked.

QUIZ QUESTIONS

Answers on page 48.

1. A football match between Leicester City and Stockport County in 1921 attracted the lowest crowd recorded for a League match. How many people watched?

2. What is the connection between Leicester and the actor John Hurt?

3. In which year did Leicester gain city status?

4. What grisly relic of punishment can be found in Leicester's Guildhall?

5. Which famous churchman died at Leicester in 1530, full of remorse?

6. When and why does legend say that a White Boar became Blue in Leicester?

7. How did Every Street get its name?

8. Where in Leicester can you find a trophy-winning cricketer, footballer and rugby player all together?

9. The popular singer Arnold George Dorsey grew up in Leicester. By what name is he better known?

10. How did the Magazine Gateway get its name?

THE HAYMARKET 1949 L144034

RECIPE

LEICESTER FISH PIE
This differs from other fish pie recipes where the fish is flaked in the sauce.

Ingredients

2lb (1kg) potatoes, peeled and cut into chunks

1½lb (750g) cod, hake or haddock fillets, skinned and cut into 4 equal pieces

Salt and pepper

1½ pints (900ml) milk

3oz (75g) butter

1½oz (40g) plain flour

Boil the potatoes in salted water until tender (15-20 minutes). Grease a wide, shallow ovenproof dish and lay the pieces of fish in it, in two layers. Season with salt and pepper, and pour over 1¼ pints (750ml) of the milk. Closely cover with foil and bake in a preheated oven for 25 minutes, 350 degrees F, 180 degrees C, Gas Mark 4.

Drain the potatoes and mash with half the butter and ¼ pint (150ml) milk, beating until soft and creamy. Leave aside to cool, but do not chill in a fridge.

Just before removing the fish from the oven, melt 1oz (25g) of the butter in a saucepan, sprinkle in the flour and cook, stirring all the time, for 1-2 minutes. Remove from the heat. Strain the cooking liquid from the fish, and gradually stir it into the butter and flour mixture. Return to the heat and cook, stirring, for 2-3 minutes, until thickened. Season to taste. Pour the sauce evenly over the fish, and leave to cool completely. When cooled, spread the mashed potato over the fish and lightly smooth over the surface, marking a decorative pattern on the top with a fork. Dot the surface with the remaining butter. Bake near the top of the preheated oven for about 25 minutes, until golden brown.

For special occasions, a luxury version of this pie can be made by stirring 3fl oz (85ml) of white wine into the roux before adding the milk, and 2 tablespoonfuls of double cream into the sauce just before pouring it over the fish.

GRANBY STREET 1949 L144035

Did You Know?
LEICESTER
A MISCELLANY

RECIPE

LEICESTERSHIRE RAREBIT

The rabbit, rare-bite, or rarebit was originally made by soaking a toasted slice of bread in front of the open fire in red wine or beer.
The thinly-cut cheese was then laid on top and left before the fire until the cheese was toasted and browned.

Ingredients

½oz (15g) butter
4oz (115g) Leicestershire cheese
2 tablespoons milk

Salt and pepper
1 teaspoonful of made mustard
Hot buttered toast

Melt the butter and add the crumbled cheese. Heat gently, stirring until melted, and gradually add the milk, doing this carefully to prevent the cheese becoming hard and lumpy. Season with salt, pepper and mustard and pour over hot buttered toast.

RECIPE

LEICESTER SAND CAKE

The use of cornflour in this delicious and unusual cake produces a light and smooth texture.

Ingredients

For cake:
3oz (75g) butter or margarine
4oz (100g) caster sugar
2 eggs, beaten
Finely grated rind of 1 lemon
4oz (100g) cornflour
1oz (25g) plain flour
1½ teaspoons baking powder

For icing:
3 teaspoons lemon juice
1 teaspoon water
4oz (100g) sifted icing sugar

Preheat the oven to 350 degrees F, 180 degrees C, Gas Mark 4. Cream the butter or margarine with the sugar until light, fluffy and pale. Gradually beat in the eggs and add the lemon rind. Sift the cornflour with the flour and baking powder, and fold into the mixture. Turn into a well-greased 1lb (450g) loaf tin. Bake in the preheated oven for about 50 minutes, or until a skewer inserted into the cake comes out clean. Turn out onto a wire rack and cool.

To make the icing, mix the lemon juice and water into the icing sugar in a small saucepan. Stir over a low heat until melted and just warm, and immediately pour over the cake and allow the icing to run down the sides. Leave to set, and serve in slices.

QUIZ ANSWERS

1. 13.

2. 50 Lee Street in Leicester was the birthplace in 1862 of Joseph Merrick, better known as the tragic Elephant Man, who was played by John Hurt in a film about Merrick's life.

3. The settlement at Leicester was mentioned in the Domesday Book as a 'civitas' (city), but Leicester lost its city status in the 11th century. It was eventually re-made a city in 1919.

4. A set of gibbet irons can be seen in Leicester's Guildhall, which were last used in 1832. They were used to display a hanged body.

5. Cardinal Wolsey, who fell from grace over the matter of Henry VIII's divorce from Katherine of Aragon, died at the Abbey of St Mary de Pratis in Leicester in 1530, whilst travelling to London to answer charges of treason. He is famous for his words of remorse about his worldly life: 'Had I but served my God as diligently as I have served my King, he would not have given me over in my gray hairs.' A slab in Abbey Park marks the presumed site of his grave.

6. A local tradition says that Richard III stayed in Leicester before the Battle of Bosworth in 1485, in an inn bearing his own emblem, the White Boar. After the battle, which resulted in the death of Richard and the triumph of Henry Tudor, (now Henry VII), the landlord quickly painted the sign blue - the Blue Boar was the emblem of the Earl of Oxford, Henry's chief supporter.

7. 'Every Street' got its name from a carrier (an early haulage/taxi business) who had a notice on the wall there claiming that he could take you to 'every street in Leicester'.

8. On the Sporting Success statue in Gallowtree Gate, which commemorates the fact that Leicester teams in the sports of cricket, football and rugby each won a major trophy in 1996; representatives from all three sports are featured on the statue.

9. Arnold George Dorsey is better known as Engelbert Humperdinck. Of Anglo Indian ethnicity, he was born on 2 May 1936 in what was then known as Madras, India, but was raised in Leicester. He adopted the stage name Engelbert Humperdinck, after the German opera composer of the same name. Engelbert received an Honorary Degree of Doctor of Music from the University of Leicester in January 2006.

10. The Magazine Gateway in the historic Old Town should really be called the Newarke Gateway, as it was the entrance to the Newarke, a 14th-century addition to Leicester Castle. However it gained the name Magazine Gateway during the Civil War, when it was used to store the town's supply of weapons and gunpowder.

THE DE MONTFORT HALL, REGENT ROAD c1955 L144118

FRANCIS FRITH

PIONEER VICTORIAN PHOTOGRAPHER

Francis Frith, founder of the world-famous photographic archive, was a complex and multi-talented man. A devout Quaker and a highly successful Victorian businessman, he was philosophical by nature and pioneering in outlook. By 1855 he had already established a wholesale grocery business in Liverpool, and sold it for the astonishing sum of £200,000, which is the equivalent today of over £15,000,000. Now in his thirties, and captivated by the new science of photography, Frith set out on a series of pioneering journeys up the Nile and to the Near East.

INTRIGUE AND EXPLORATION

He was the first photographer to venture beyond the sixth cataract of the Nile. Africa was still the mysterious 'Dark Continent', and Stanley and Livingstone's historic meeting was a decade into the future. The conditions for picture taking confound belief. He laboured for hours in his wicker dark-room in the sweltering heat of the desert, while the volatile chemicals fizzed dangerously in their trays. Back in London he exhibited his photographs and was 'rapturously cheered' by members of the Royal Society. His reputation as a photographer was made overnight.

VENTURE OF A LIFE-TIME

By the 1870s the railways had threaded their way across the country, and Bank Holidays and half-day Saturdays had been made obligatory by Act of Parliament. All of a sudden the working man and his family were able to enjoy days out, take holidays, and see a little more of the world.

With typical business acumen, Francis Frith foresaw that these new tourists would enjoy having souvenirs to commemorate their days out. For the next thirty years he travelled the country by train and by pony and trap, producing fine photographs of seaside resorts and beauty spots that were keenly bought by millions of Victorians. These prints were painstakingly pasted into family albums and pored over during the dark nights of winter, rekindling precious memories of summer excursions. Frith's studio was soon supplying retail shops all over the country, and by 1890 F Frith & Co had become the greatest specialist photographic publishing company in the world, with over 2,000 sales outlets, and pioneered the picture postcard.

FRANCIS FRITH'S LEGACY

Francis Frith had died in 1898 at his villa in Cannes, his great project still growing. By 1970 the archive he created contained over a third of a million pictures showing 7,000 British towns and villages.

Frith's legacy to us today is of immense significance and value, for the magnificent archive of evocative photographs he created provides a unique record of change in the cities, towns and villages throughout Britain over a century and more. Frith and his fellow studio photographers revisited locations many times down the years to update their views, compiling for us an enthralling and colourful pageant of British life and character.

We are fortunate that Frith was dedicated to recording the minutiae of everyday life. For it is this sheer wealth of visual data, the painstaking chronicle of changes in dress, transport, street layouts, buildings, housing and landscape that captivates us so much today, offering us a powerful link with the past and with the lives of our ancestors.

Computers have now made it possible for Frith's many thousands of images to be accessed almost instantly. The archive offers every one of us an opportunity to examine the places where we and our families have lived and worked down the years. Its images, depicting our shared past, are now bringing pleasure and enlightenment to millions around the world a century and more after his death.

For further information visit: www.francisfrith.com

INTERIOR DECORATION

Frith's photographs can be seen framed and as giant wall murals in thousands of pubs, restaurants, hotels, banks, retail stores and other public buildings throughout Britain. These provide interesting and attractive décor, generating strong local interest and acting as a powerful reminder of gentler days in our increasingly busy and frenetic world.

FRITH PRODUCTS

All Frith photographs are available as prints and posters in a variety of different sizes and styles. In the UK we also offer a range of other gift and stationery products illustrated with Frith photographs, although many of these are not available for delivery outside the UK – see our web site for more information on the products available for delivery in your country.

THE INTERNET

Over 100,000 photographs of Britain can be viewed and purchased on the Frith web site. The web site also includes memories and reminiscences contributed by our customers, who have personal knowledge of localities and of the people and properties depicted in Frith photographs. If you wish to learn more about a specific town or village you may find these reminiscences fascinating to browse. Why not add your own comments if you think they would be of interest to others? See **www.francisfrith.com**

PLEASE HELP US BRING FRITH'S PHOTOGRAPHS TO LIFE

Our authors do their best to recount the history of the places they write about. They give insights into how particular towns and villages developed, they describe the architecture of streets and buildings, and they discuss the lives of famous people who lived there. But however knowledgeable our authors are, the story they tell is necessarily incomplete.

Frith's photographs are so much more than plain historical documents. They are living proofs of the flow of human life down the generations. They show real people at real moments in history; and each of those people is the son or daughter of someone, the brother or sister, aunt or uncle, grandfather or grandmother of someone else. All of them lived, worked and played in the streets depicted in Frith's photographs.

We would be grateful if you would give us your insights into the places shown in our photographs: the streets and buildings, the shops, businesses and industries. Post your memories of life in those streets on the Frith website: what it was like growing up there, who ran the local shop and what shopping was like years ago; if your workplace is shown tell us about your working day and what the building is used for now. Read other visitors' memories and reconnect with your shared local history and heritage. With your help more and more Frith photographs can be brought to life, and vital memories preserved for posterity, and for the benefit of historians in the future.

Wherever possible, we will try to include some of your comments in future editions of our books. Moreover, if you spot errors in dates, titles or other facts, please let us know, because our archive records are not always completely accurate—they rely on 140 years of human endeavour and hand-compiled records. You can email us using the contact form on the website.

Thank you!

For further information, trade, or author enquiries please contact us at the address below:

The Francis Frith Collection, Frith's Barn, Teffont, Salisbury, Wiltshire, England SP3 5QP.

Tel: +44 (0)1722 716 376 Fax: +44 (0)1722 716 881
e-mail: sales@francisfrith.co.uk **www.francisfrith.com**